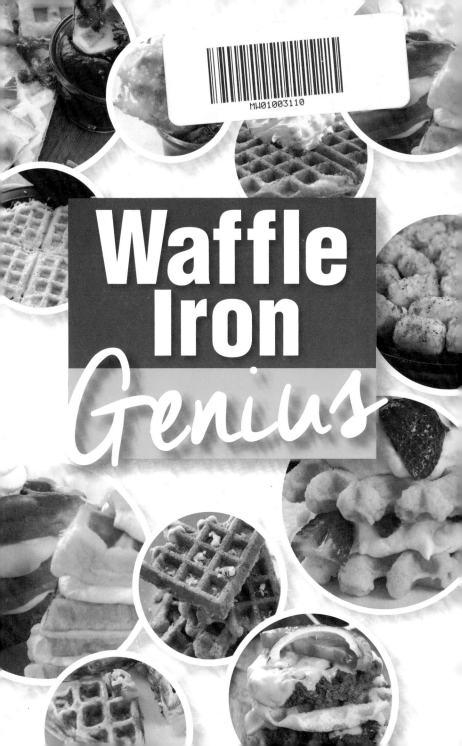

Waffle
Iron
Genius

NOT ALL WAFFLE IRONS ARE CREATED EQUAL

So these recipes don't include cooking times. But don't panic–for most, you'll know the waffled food is done when your iron's indicator light comes on *(but in some cases, the food will need a little bit more time)*. Just peek inside once you start smelling deliciousness.

Printed in the United States of America
by G&R Publishing Co.

Distributed By:

Products

507 Industrial Street
Waverly, IA 50677

ISBN-13: 978-1-56383-512-4
Item #7112

Waffle Wisdom

Know your waffle iron

Check the owner's manual for your waffle iron to gauge the amount of batter to use. But remember, you're not dealing with actual waffle batter here, so you might need to use a little more or less batter for some recipes.

The argument for grease

Most waffle irons have a nonstick surface, but greasing your iron anyway will help prevent any unexpected mishaps. Using a light coating of vegetable oil works well.

Browning factor

Some of the recipes will indicate a specific cooking temperature. If your waffle iron doesn't have a browning control setting, just cook the food until it's done to your liking. When cooking thicker food, you may want to flip the food to promote all-over browning.

Keep it clean

Again, refer to your owner's manual when cleaning your waffle iron, but always unplug the iron and let it cool before you clean it. A plastic bristle brush or a nylon mesh pad works well for getting into those grooves.

Let's Waffle!

APPLE BREAD

1½ C. flour

¾ tsp. ground cinnamon

½ tsp. baking soda

⅛ tsp. baking powder

½ tsp. salt

1 egg plus 1 egg white

1 C. sugar

½ C. vegetable oil

1½ tsp. vanilla

1 C. finely chopped Golden Delicious apple *(peeled)*

¼ C. finely chopped walnuts

Steps

In a small bowl, mix flour, cinnamon, baking soda, baking powder, and salt. In a medium bowl, beat egg and egg white; add sugar and oil and beat until well blended. Stir in vanilla and the flour mixture. The batter will be thick. Toss the apple and walnuts in the mix and give it a good stir. Now you're ready to waffle it.

Preheat your waffle iron and coat lightly with oil.

Pour some batter onto the hot iron, close the lid, and bake until done.

Drizzle with a little melted butter and this bread will simply melt in your mouth.

No need to heat up your oven – this may easily become your favorite way to make bread.

EGGPLANT PARM

Serves 1

¼ C. flour

½ tsp. pepper

2 tsp. salt, divided

1 egg, beaten

½ C. dry Italian bread crumbs

¼ C. cornmeal

1 T. grated Parmesan cheese

1 eggplant, sliced into ½" rounds

Cooked pasta

Pasta sauce

Shredded cheese *(we used an Italian Cheese blend)*

Steps

In a bowl, stir together the flour, pepper, and 1 teaspoon salt.

In another bowl, whisk together egg and ¼ cup water until well blended.

In a third bowl, combine the bread crumbs, cornmeal, Parmesan cheese, and remaining 1 teaspoon salt; stir to blend.

Preheat and grease your waffle iron.

Dip both sides of eggplant rounds into the flour mixture, then the egg, and then the bread crumb mixture. Arrange a few of them on the hot iron, set the lid down gently, and cook until toasty brown. Repeat with remaining rounds *(may need to cook for a few minutes after the iron's indicator light comes on)*.

Serve with hot cooked pasta, sauce, and shredded cheese.

TATER TOT FLATS

Onion-flavored tater tots, thawed

¼ tsp. dried parsley flakes

¼ tsp. seasoned salt

¼ tsp. dry mustard

¼ tsp. pepper

How do you like your tater tots? If you like 'em hot, brown, and crispy, you've come to the right place. Behold the power of the waffle iron.

Steps

Preheat and lightly grease your waffle iron *(if your iron has a browning control setting, set it on high)*.

Coat the tater tots with a good spritz of cooking spray.

Stir together the parsley flakes, seasoned salt, dry mustard, and pepper; sprinkle evenly over the tots.

Arrange tots close together in the iron. Set the lid down gently and bake until deep brown and crispy, pressing down lightly on the handle occasionally so the tots in the front get done *(use a hot pad)*.

Serves 2

WHY WAFFLE IT?

It's a crunch fest in here! You get all the crunch, all the way through. And the seasoning mix just makes 'em even more **scrumptious!**

APPLE TART

1 puff pastry sheet, thawed

1 baking apple *(we used Gala)*

1½ tsp. ground cinnamon, divided

2 T. sugar, divided

3 T. chopped pecans

Frosting

Steps

Coat your waffle iron lightly with oil, but don't preheat it. Cut the thawed pastry to fit and set piece(s) on the cold iron.

Core the apple and thinly slice it into a medium bowl. Mix the cinnamon and sugar and sprinkle about half of it over the apples; stir to coat and set the remaining cinnamon-sugar aside. Divide the apple slices among your pastry pieces, arranging them in a single layer; sprinkle the pecans over the apples.

Go ahead and close the lid right over the apples and plug in the iron *(be brave – it'll work)*. When it's a beautiful shade of golden brown and the pastry is cooked *(may need to cook several minutes after the indicator light comes on)*, remove from the iron. Sprinkle with some of the remaining cinnamon-sugar. Repeat with all of the pastry pieces.

Warm the frosting and drizzle it over each pastry.

PARMESAN CRISPS

1½ C. shredded Parmesan cheese

1 T. flour

2 tsp. chopped fresh basil or oregano

Steps

Lightly grease your waffle iron and preheat it *(if your iron has a browning control setting, set it on medium-high).*

Toss the cheese with the flour until coated. Then stir in the basil. That's it!

Make a mound of the cheese mixture *(about 2 tablespoons)* on each section of the iron. Close the lid and cook until they're brown and baked to beautiful perfection. *(These will lift easily out of the iron, and the little cheesy bits that get left behind are yummy, too.)*

Dip into marinara sauce for extra Italian flair, if you'd like.

Crisp-edged, golden brown, mmm-mmm goodness!

Garden Veggie Calzones

¼ C. shredded carrots

½ C. thinly sliced mushrooms

½ C. thinly sliced zucchini

½ C. finely chopped red bell pepper

¼ C. finely chopped red onion

½ tsp. garlic salt

½ tsp. pepper

Fresh basil to taste

1 (13.8 oz.) tube refrigerated pizza crust dough *(we used artisan-style)*

4 oz. fresh mozzarella cheese, thinly sliced

Steps

Grease your waffle iron, but don't preheat it.

In a large bowl, mix the carrots, mushrooms, zucchini, bell pepper, onion, garlic salt, and pepper.

Thinly roll out the pizza dough and cut into pieces to fit on the iron. Set one piece on the cold iron. Place about half the veggie mixture and half the cheese in a thin, even layer over the dough. Add basil and set a second piece of dough on top. Set the lid down gently and plug in the iron.

Cook until nicely browned, pressing down lightly on the handle occasionally so the dough in the front gets done. **Serves 6**

SWITCH IT UP

Switch out any of the filling ingredients with your favorites. Want meat? Add it. Cheese only? No problem. Asparagus in the spring, squash in the fall? You bet – try 'em all!

STRAWBERRY SHORTS

Serves 6

1½ lbs. fresh strawberries, sliced

½ C. sugar, divided

2 C. flour

2 tsp. baking powder

¼ tsp. baking soda

⅛ tsp. salt

3 C. whipping cream, divided

1½ tsp. clear vanilla

Steps

Mix the berries with 3 tablespoons sugar and refrigerate at least ½ hour.

Sift together the flour, baking powder, baking soda, salt, and 2 tablespoons sugar. Add 1½ cups of the whipping cream and stir until just combined. Batter will be thick!

Preheat and grease your waffle iron.

Place ¼-cup mounds of batter on the iron, close the lid, and cook until brown. Remove from the iron and set on a wire rack to cool.

Beat remaining 1½ cups of whipping cream, remaining 3 tablespoons sugar, and vanilla until soft peaks form.

Layer shortcakes, berries and juice, and whipping cream.

CHEESY OMELETS

Serves 1

4 eggs

2 T. half & half

6 fully cooked bacon strips, crumbled

½ C. shredded cheese *(we used sharp Cheddar)*

¼ C. chopped tomato

3 green onions, sliced

Salt & pepper to taste

Steps

Preheat and lightly grease your waffle iron.

In a bowl, whisk together the eggs and half & half until well blended. Stir in bacon, cheese, tomato, green onions, salt, and pepper.

Pour part of the mixture onto the hot iron, close the lid, and cook until the eggs are done to your liking.

Tip: The longer the eggs are in the iron, the easier it is to remove them.

For real confusion at the table, serve these with waffles!

Thanksgiving Leftovers

4 C. leftover stuffing *(or prepared Stovetop Stuffing)*

½ C. finely diced celery

1 C. shredded or diced cooked turkey

½ C. dried cranberries

Chicken broth, optional

Steps

Preheat and lightly grease your waffle iron.

Stir together stuffing, celery, turkey, and dried cranberries until well blended. If your mixture is dry, stir in a bit of chicken broth or water *(you want it to hold together just a bit)*. Pack an even layer of the stuffing mixture onto your iron *(and really fill those corners, too)*. Close the lid and cook until nicely browned and crisp. **Serves 6**

You can waffle your leftover mashed potatoes, too (page 44).

CHECK THIS OUT

Don't cover the dividers in your iron with stuffing – it's easier to remove if you have smaller portions. Customize your stuffing by adding chopped fresh mushrooms, pine nuts, or extra herbs, if you'd like. Serve with cranberry sauce or gravy, too!

PIZZA POCKETS

Serves 8

1 (16.3 oz.) tube refrigerated Grands Flaky Layers Buttermilk biscuits

Pizza sauce

Pizza toppings *(we used mini pepperoni, green bell pepper, mushrooms & chives)*

Shredded cheese *(we used an Italian cheese blend)*

Steps

Preheat and lightly grease your waffle iron.

Simply cut a pocket into the side of each biscuit and stuff with topping ingredients; press edges to seal the topping safely inside. Put a few on the iron; set the lid down gently, and cook until toasty brown, pressing down lightly on the handle occasionally so the dough in the front gets done *(use a hot pad).*

Serve with a side of pizza sauce for dipping, if you'd like.

Change up the filling ingredients and you can have made-to-order pizzas any night of the week.

ALOHA QUESADILLAS

Flour tortillas

Shredded cheese *(we used a Mexican cheese blend)*

Crushed pineapple, drained

Red onion, chopped

Canadian bacon slices or cooked, crumbled bacon

BBQ sauce

Steps

Lightly grease your waffle iron, but don't preheat it.

Lay one tortilla on the cold iron. Add thin layers of cheese, pineapple, onion, and Canadian bacon. Drizzle with a little BBQ sauce and set another tortilla on top.

Plug in the iron, close the lid, and cook until the little pockets made by the iron are light golden brown.

Serve with extra BBQ sauce and maybe a little sour cream for good measure.

FAUX FRY HODGE PODGE

Assorted fresh veggies *(we used mushrooms, zucchini, dill pickles, onion & bell pepper)*

1 C. milk

2 T. distilled white vinegar

1½ T. vegetable oil

1¼ to 1½ C. flour

1 tsp. baking powder

1 tsp. salt

¼ tsp. cayenne pepper

1 tsp. garlic salt

½ tsp. dill weed

Steps

Cut veggies into desired shapes that are all about the same thickness. Remove excess moisture by blotting with paper towels; set aside.

Stir together the milk, vinegar, oil, flour, baking powder, salt, cayenne pepper, garlic salt, and dill weed until well blended.

Grease and preheat your waffle iron *(if your iron has a browning control setting, set it on high)*.

Dip veggies partway into batter and remove excess. Place on hot iron, close the lid, and cook until golden brown. Enjoy immediately.

Serve with dipping sauce of your choice. **Servings vary**

WHY WAFFLE IT?

No deep fryer oil splatters messing up your nice clean kitchen. Without all that oil, they're healthier, too!

27

S'MOREFFLES

2 T. butter, melted

2 tsp. sugar

2 tsp. powdered sugar

1 C. milk

1 egg

⅔ C. flour

1 tsp. baking powder

¼ tsp. salt

2 T. unsweetened
   cocoa powder

3 T. graham cracker crumbs

Mini marshmallows

Mini semi-sweet
   chocolate chips

Steps

In a bowl, beat together butter, sugar, powdered sugar, milk, and egg. Sift flour, baking powder, salt, and cocoa into butter mixture. Add cracker crumbs and beat until well blended. The batter will be thin. Let set 25 to 30 minutes.

Preheat and grease your waffle iron.

Pour enough batter on the iron to just cover the bottom. Close the lid and cook until just barely crisp.

Open the lid and put a handful of marshmallows and some chocolate chips over the front half of the S'moreffle. Carefully fold the back half over the filling and gently close the lid for a few seconds until the filling starts to melt. Remove and repeat with remaining batter.

Watch out – that gooey filling is hot!

Spinach Wontons

Stir together 1 (8 oz.) pkg. cream cheese *(softened)*, 1 (10 oz.) pkg. frozen spinach *(thawed and squeezed dry)*, ½ tsp. garlic salt, ½ tsp. coarse black pepper, and a pinch of cayenne pepper. Preheat and grease your waffle iron. Place 2 to 3 tsp. of spinach mixture on each of 24 wonton wrappers; wet the edges of the wrappers with water and fold in half, pressing edges to seal. Set on the hot iron; close and cook until nicely browned. Enjoy immediately.
Serves 24

Quick Cinnamon Rolls

Preheat and grease your waffle iron. Place a few individual rolls from a tube of refrigerated cinnamon rolls on the hot iron; close and cook until golden brown and no longer doughy. Repeat with remaining rolls. Spread with frosting. **Serves 8**

Mini Muffin Crisps

Whip up a batch of muffins from a mix *(or your favorite recipe)*. Drop batter by tablespoon onto a hot greased waffle iron. Close and cook until muffins are done. Spread softened butter over the top of hot muffin crisps so you can enjoy all those little pools of melted goodness. **Servings vary**

Easy Cherry Turnovers

Preheat and grease your waffle iron. Assemble refrigerated fill-and-bake turnovers as directed on package. Set a couple of turnovers on the hot iron, close, and cook until golden brown and no longer doughy. Repeat with remaining turnovers. Drizzle with frosting. **Serves 6**

BANANA BITES

½ C. flour

½ C. cornstarch

⅓ C. sweetened flaked *(or toasted)* coconut

2 T. sugar

½ tsp. baking powder

Pinch of salt

2 egg yolks

¼ C. plus 1T. milk

¼ tsp. vanilla

7 firm bananas, divided

Steps

Stir together the flour, cornstarch, coconut, sugar, baking powder, and salt. Add egg yolks, milk, and vanilla. Mash one banana and stir it into the mixture.

Preheat and lightly grease your waffle iron.

Peel one banana; slice in half crosswise and then slice each half lengthwise *(you'll have four banana pieces)*. Dunk each piece into the batter and remove excess. Place the pieces on the hot iron, close the lid, and cook until toasty brown and edges are cooked. Repeat with remaining bananas.

Serve with syrup and/or honey on the side, if you'd like. **Serves 6**

NOW TRY THIS

If you have batter remaining, just place small mounds of the batter in the waffle iron and cook until done. They'll still taste great, with a hint of banana flavor.

MONTE CRISTO

4 Bagel Thins

Mustard

Mayo

Deli sliced turkey

Deli sliced ham

Swiss cheese slices

1 egg

About ½ C. milk

Steps

Preheat your waffle iron.

For each sandwich, spread the cut sides of a bagel thin with mustard and mayo. To the coated side of one half, add thin layers of turkey, ham, and cheese. Place the other bagel half on top, cut side down.

In a small bowl, beat together the egg and milk until well combined. Dip both sides of one sandwich in the egg mixture and place on the hot iron. Close the lid and press down lightly on the handle. Cook until toasted to your liking. Repeat with remaining sandwiches.

CARROT CAKE

2 C. sugar

1 C. vegetable oil

4 eggs

2 C. flour

½ tsp. salt

1 tsp. baking soda

1 tsp. baking powder

1 tsp. ground cinnamon

2 C. grated carrots

Chopped pecans to taste

Your favorite cream cheese frosting

Luscious Layers

Steps

Beat together the sugar, oil, and eggs.

In a separate bowl, stir together the dry ingredients; add to the egg mixture and stir in the carrots until well blended.

Preheat and grease your waffle iron.

Pour batter onto the iron, close the lid, and cook until golden brown. Remove and set on a wire rack to cool.

Stir the pecans into the frosting and spread over your cooled cakes.

WAFFLE-STYLE CORN DOGS

1 C. flour

½ C. yellow cornmeal

1 T. sugar

1 T. baking powder

1 tsp. salt

½ tsp. dry mustard

¼ tsp. paprika

¼ tsp. black pepper

1 egg

1 to 1¼ C. evaporated milk

10 small or regular hot dogs
   (not Plumpers)

Steps

Stir together the dry ingredients. Mix in egg and 1 cup evaporated milk until well blended, adding the remaining ¼ cup milk to reach dipping consistency, if needed. Transfer batter to a tall drinking glass.

Preheat and lightly grease your waffle iron.

Pat hot dogs dry and insert a bamboo skewer lengthwise through the center of each. Dip each hot dog into the batter, swirl, and lift. You'll want a fairly thin coating of batter, so gently remove excess.

Place a couple of the hot dogs on the hot iron, set the lid down gently, and cook until no longer doughy.

Enjoy immediately. **Serves 10**

TRY THIS INSTEAD

If you don't have skewers, you can just slice 8 to 10 small hot dogs and stir them into the batter. Pour batter in batches onto the greased iron, close the lid, and cook until done.

LASAGNA FOLDS

Serves 6

6 uncooked lasagna noodles

½ C. ricotta cheese

½ tsp. minced garlic

1 egg yolk, beaten

½ tsp. salt

¼ tsp. pepper

Vegetable oil

6 oz. Italian sausage, cooked, drained & crumbled

½ (10 oz.) pkg. frozen chopped spinach, thawed & squeezed dry

½ C. shredded cheese *(we used Colby-Jack)*, plus more for sprinkling

Marinara sauce

Steps

Cook noodles according to package directions until nearly done; drain the pasta and drizzle with a little oil. Stir together ricotta cheese, garlic, egg yolk, salt, and pepper.

Preheat and grease your waffle iron.

Lay the noodles side by side on a flat surface. Divide the ricotta cheese mixture, sausage, spinach, and shredded cheese evenly among the noodles, covering only half of each noodle with the mixture. Drizzle each with a little marinara sauce. Fold the plain half of each noodle over the filling. Carefully move one or two of the filled noodles to the iron and set the lid down gently. Cook until noodles are just beginning to brown and the filling is bubbly.

Remove from the iron and serve with extra marinara sauce and a little extra cheese if you'd like.

DESSERT CHIMICHANGAS

Makes 6

¾ C. sugar

2¼ tsp. ground cinnamon

1¾ C. ready-to-eat cheesecake filling

1 C. coarsely chopped fresh strawberries and/or blueberries

6 (8") flour tortillas

Nonstick cooking spray

Steps

Combine the sugar and cinnamon on a plate or pie plate and stir until it's nicely blended together; set aside.

Lightly grease your waffle iron and preheat it *(if your iron has a browning control setting, set it on medium-high).*

Stir together the cheesecake filling and the berries. Divide the mixture evenly among the tortillas, putting the filling near the bottom of each and spreading it out ever-so slightly. Fold in the sides and roll each one up like a burrito.

Coat the outside of one tortilla roll with cooking spray and set it on the hot iron. Close the iron lightly and cook until it's toasty brown *(you may want to flip it over at this point so the front and back become evenly browned).* Remove it from the iron, coat the outside again with cooking spray, and roll it in the cinnamon-sugar mixture so it's evenly coated. Now just repeat with the remaining tortillas.

A little bit crunchy and a whole lot delicious!

CHEESE-STUDDED MASHERS

¼ C. butter, melted

¼ C. buttermilk

2 eggs

2 C. leftover mashed
potatoes

2 T. chopped fresh chives

½ C. flour

½ tsp. baking powder

½ tsp. salt

½ tsp. pepper

¼ tsp. baking soda

¼ tsp. garlic powder

1 C. shredded cheese *(we
used Colby)*

Steps

Whisk together butter, buttermilk, and eggs until well combined. Add the mashed potatoes and chives. Stir gently until blended.

In a separate bowl, stir together all of the dry ingredients and the cheese. Add this mixture to the buttermilk mixture and stir, but don't over-mix *(you just want the dry ingredients to disappear)*.

Preheat and lightly grease your waffle iron.

Drop potatoes in ⅓-cup mounds, close the lid, and bake until golden brown and slightly crispy *(may need to cook for a few minutes after the iron's indicator light comes on)*.

Garnish and serve any way you'd like. Some extra chives for color? Why not! **Serves 8**

WHY WAFFLE IT?

These potatoes are crunchy on the outside, soft on the inside. *It's potato perfection!*

45

Bacon & Avocado

For each sandwich, butter one side of two ¼"-thick ciabatta bread slices. On the unbuttered side of one, stack thin slices of avocado and cooked bacon; sprinkle with shredded Colby cheese. Place the other bread slice on top, buttered side out. Place on a hot waffle iron, close, and cook until perfectly toasted. **Serves 1**

Chicken & Steak Fries

Thaw frozen chicken strips and seasoned steak fries. Pop them onto a hot waffle iron, close, and cook until heated through. *(You can cook them together if your chicken strips and fries are uniform in thickness; otherwise, it's best to cook them separately.)* **Servings vary**

Reubens

For each sandwich, spread one side of two rye bread slices with thousand island dressing. To the coated side of one slice, add thin layers of Swiss cheese, pastrami or corned beef, and sauerkraut *(drained and squeezed to remove excess moisture)*. Put the other bread slice on top, coated side in. Butter the outsides, set on a hot waffle iron, close, and cook until golden brown. **Serves 1**

Triple Cheese

For each sandwich, butter one side of two bread slices. On the unbuttered side of one, layer your favorite cheeses *(we used American, Swiss, and Gouda on multi-grain bread)*. Don't be shy – really pile that cheese on there! Place the other bread slice on top, buttered side out. Set on a hot waffle iron, close, and cook until toasty. **Serves 1**

GLAZED DONUT DIPPERS

Serves 8

½ C. sugar

2 tsp. baking powder

¾ tsp. salt

¼ tsp. ground nutmeg

1 egg

½ C. plus 2 T. milk, divided

2 T. butter, melted

1½ C. flour

¾ C. powdered sugar

1 tsp. vanilla, almond, lemon, or orange flavoring

Decorating sprinkles

Steps

Stir together the sugar, baking powder, salt, and nutmeg. Add the egg, ½ cup milk, and butter; beat well. Stir in flour, mixing until thoroughly combined. Batter will be thick.

Preheat and grease your waffle iron.

Scoop batter onto hot iron, close the lid, and cook until golden brown. Remove from iron and set on a wire rack to cool. Repeat with remaining batter.

Stir together powdered sugar, remaining 2 tablespoons milk, and flavoring until smooth. Dip donuts into glaze. Return to rack and toss on some decorating sprinkles.

CRAB CAKES

1 (8 oz.) pkg. imitation crabmeat

1 egg white

2 T. mayo

¾ tsp. Dijon mustard

½ to ¾ tsp. Old Bay seasoning

½ tsp. lemon juice

¼ tsp. Worcestershire sauce

¼ tsp. salt

½ C. plus 2 T. fresh bread crumbs from soft white sandwich bread

1½ tsp. chopped fresh parsley

Steps

Place the crabmeat in a bowl and gently break apart. In a separate bowl, whisk together the egg white, mayo, mustard, seasoning, lemon juice, Worcestershire sauce, and salt. Add egg mixture to the crabmeat and stir gently without over-mixing. Toss in the bread crumbs and parsley; mix gently. Cover with plastic wrap and refrigerate 1 hour.

Preheat and lightly grease your waffle iron.

Drop heaping tablespoons of the chilled crab mixture onto the hot iron. Close the lid and cook a few minutes until nicely browned.

Serve with fruit salsa or your favorite seafood dipping sauce.
Serves 6

TRY THIS INSTEAD

How about making tuna patties? Just replace crabmeat with 1 (7 oz.) pouch of tuna. Mix and cook as directed above.

CHEESEBURGERS

1 lb. lean ground beef

Seasonings of your choice

Cheese slices *(we used American)*

Butter, softened

5 hamburger buns

Steps

Preheat and lightly grease your waffle iron.

Shape beef into five patties, season them as you like, and set them on the hot iron. Close the lid and cook until patties are done the way you like them. Surprise – they'll be cooked to perfection in minutes!

Add a slice of cheese to each burger and remove from the iron.

Butter the cut side of each bun, put them on the iron, and set the lid down gently on them. Cook for a minute or so until they're toasty.

When your burger and bun are "waffled," it just makes everything a little extra fun.

ICE CREAM SANDWICHES

Serves 12

1 C. sugar

½ C. butter, softened

2 eggs

½ C. half & half

1¾ C. flour

1 tsp. baking powder

½ C. unsweetened
  cocoa powder

½ tsp. salt

1 tsp. vanilla

Ice cream (we used mint-
  chocolate chip)

Steps

Mix the sugar and butter until creamy. Add the eggs, beating until well blended. Add the half & half, flour, baking powder, cocoa, salt, and vanilla; mix well.

Preheat and grease your waffle iron.

Drop tablespoons of dough on the hot iron, close the lid, and cook until the steaming stops. Peek in there – they should be done. Remove them to a wire rack and repeat with remaining dough.

When they're cool, fill them with ice cream and serve immediately. Or wrap individually in plastic wrap and store in the freezer for later.

Slicing a block of ice cream and then cutting to fit the cookies makes them easy to fill.

CINNAMON FRENCH TOAST

2 eggs	1½ tsp. sugar
⅓ C. milk	¼ tsp. cinnamon
½ tsp. vanilla	6 bread slices

How do you like French Toast? With syrup and fruit? Butter and honey? Sour cream and jam? Who's hungry?

Steps

Preheat and lightly grease your waffle iron.

Whisk together eggs, milk, vanilla, sugar, and cinnamon until very well blended.

One at a time, dip bread slices in the egg mixture and place on the iron. Close the lid and bake until golden brown.

Serve this French toast your favorite way. **Serves 3**

WHY WAFFLE IT?

No more soggy French toast. The waffle iron takes care of that wiggly-jiggly too-soft middle, and you're left with the nice texture of this toast. Try using French bread, cinnamon swirl bread, or any other bread you enjoy.

LEMON CAKES

1 (15.25 oz.) pkg. lemon cake mix

Water, oil & eggs as directed
    on cake mix pkg.

1 T. lemon flavoring, divided

2 C. whipping cream

2 T. sugar

Zest of 1 lemon

Steps

Stir together cake mix, water, oil, and eggs as directed on cake mix package, adding 1 teaspoon lemon flavoring.

Preheat and grease your waffle iron.

Pour batter on the iron, close the lid, and cook until light golden brown. Set on a wire rack to cool. Repeat with remaining batter.

Beat together the whipping cream, sugar, lemon zest, and remaining 2 teaspoons flavoring on high speed until soft peaks form.

Serve cake with whipped cream.

Mix and match other cakes and flavorings to suit your mood and to make your taste buds happy.

BEER-BATTERED SHRIMP

Serves 8

1 (12 oz.) can of beer

2 C. flour

1 tsp. garlic powder

1½ tsp. salt

1 tsp. black pepper

¾ to 1 tsp. cayenne pepper

About 2 lbs. peeled & deveined
cooked shrimp, thawed

Steps

Whisk together beer, flour, garlic powder, salt, black pepper,
and cayenne pepper until smooth.

Preheat and grease your waffle iron.

Dunk shrimp in the batter and remove excess. Arrange
several shrimp on the iron and close the lid. Cook until batter
is light golden brown and no longer doughy. Peek in on them
every now and then to see how they're doing *(may need to
cook several minutes after the indicator light comes on)*.

Drizzle with lemon juice and dunk into your favorite sauce,
if desired.

BUFFALOED CHICKEN

½ C. shredded cooked chicken

2½ T. wing sauce

1½ T. mayo

1 T. grated carrot

2 T. finely chopped celery

2 T. thinly sliced green onion

2 T. blue cheese crumbles

2 T. shredded Cheddar cheese

Butter

4 slices ciabatta bread, about ⅜" thick

Steps

Preheat your waffle iron.

Stir together the chicken, wing sauce, mayo, carrot, celery, and green onion.

Spread the mixture on two slices of bread. Sprinkle with both kinds of cheese and top each with a second bread slice.

Butter the outside of each bread slice and set on the hot iron. Close the lid and cook until golden brown and crisp.

Serve with wing sauce, if you'd like. **Serves 2**

Dips and crevices make wonderful places for extra wing sauce!

TRY THIS INSTEAD

Ranch dressing has a cooling effect on buffaloed chicken. So go ahead and serve these sandwiches with a side of dressing instead of wing sauce for dipping. Or dip them in both for a blast of hot AND cool.

INDEX